United We Stand

UNITED WE STAND

A TRIBUTE TO THE AMERICAN FALLEN HEROES OF THE WAR ON TERRORISM

EUGENE L. WEEMS

Most Trafford titles are also available at major online book retailers.

Note for Librarians: A cataloguing record for this book is available from Library
and Archives Canada at www.collectionscanada.ca/amicus/index-e.html

Printed in Victoria, BC, Canada.

ISBN: 978-1-4251-9130-6 (sc)

ISBN: 978-1-4269-0294-9 (e-book)

*We at Trafford believe that it is the responsibility of us all, as both individuals
and corporations, to make choices that are environmentally and socially sound.
You, in turn, are supporting this responsible conduct each time you purchase a
Trafford book, or make use of our publishing services. To find out how you are
helping, please visit www.trafford.com/responsiblepublishing.html*

*Our mission is to efficiently provide the world's finest, most comprehensive
book publishing service, enabling every author to experience success.
To find out how to publish your book, your way, and have it available
worldwide, visit us online at www.trafford.com*

Trafford rev.5/20/2009

Trafford
PUBLISHING®   www.trafford.com

North America & international
toll-free: 1 888 232 4444 (USA & Canada)
phone: 250 383 6864 ♦ fax: 250 383 6804 ♦ email: info@trafford.com

The United Kingdom & Europe
phone: +44 (0)1865 487 395 ♦ local rate: 0845 230 9601
facsimile: +44 (0)1865 481 507 ♦ email: info.uk@trafford.com

10 9 8 7 6 5 4 3 2 1

Illustrations by Eugene Weems

DEDICATION

To our U.S. Military Armed Forces personnel, both living and deceased. Truly you are the elements that make the United States of America the land of the free. For protecting our liberty, safety, and dignity from the enemies while standing strong for our nation's creed.

Written words and spoken sentiments are only a fragment of my appreciation, but must suffice for the contribution that has been rendered by you for this nation. Surely you are appreciated and never forgotten, and the core of my heart and support are with you.

This book is dedicated to you heroes.

ACKNOWLEDGEMENTS

To Aldine Weems, Larae Weems, Annie Montgomery, Nadine Montgomery, Henry Ridley Sr., Henry Ridley Jr., Larry Bolden, Bee Johnson, Timothy Blackburn, Tiana Blackburn, Tiara Blackburn, Sophia Lim, James Weems, Larry Weems and Robert Swain, you all are dearly remembered.

I'd like to express special thanks to God, Aunt Betty Ridley, my friends Demetrius McClendon, and Kimberlaine Johnson to whom I am indebted for their contributions, support and assistance in creating this wonderful memorial book that is dedicated to our American soldiers and fallen heroes of the war on terrorism. I truly do appreciate the patience and encouragement I've received from you on this project.

Much love to Leonard Weems, Steven Ridley, Debbie Ridley, Gwendolyn James, Kishana Weems, Lamond Moore, Eugene Johnson, Michelle Payton, Michael & Yolanda Jacobs, Kisha Gray, Sparkle Jacobs, Sheila Devereaux, Threathere Pickett, Curtis Schuler, Ruby Duncan, Nakesha Whittle, Qureonta Whittle, Delbert Smith, Demond Hammond, David Phillips, Gena Johnson, Corey Miller, Julian Walker, Elizabeth Hall, Roxie Ann Deku, George Morillo, Chi Ali Griffith, Milkman, D-Shot, Spice-1, E-40, Suga-T, 702, Kwame Teague, Ellen Wicklum, Kwobena Hobbs, Sabrina Green, Heather Hall and to all my other family and friends I haven t named.

Most importantly I'd like to express a super, super thanks to the American military armed forces

ii

personnel for their contributions and sacrifices for their country. Their love and loyalty is unconditional; likewise my appreciation, support, respect and love for them.

Sincerely,
Mr. Eugene L. Weems
Las Vegas, Nevada
Author of Prison Secrets

The Author and his Friends

ABOUT THE AUTHOR

Eugene Weems was born and raised in Las Vegas, Nevada, and is a former five-time Toughman Champion and two-time Underground Cage Fighting Champion and has been a member of the World TaeKwondo Federation and Muay Thai Kickboxing Federation since 1988.

Weems is a clothing designer, producer, mentor, business consultant, party thrower, actor, model, dancer, poet, novelist, essayist, short story and screen play writer and author of Prison Secrets. Among his many talents, he has been a life-long and tireless advocate for kids and at-risk youth.

He utilizes hip-hop and traditional elements to reach out to the youth and gangs in hope to deviate them from negative thinking and objectives.

Weems is an expert in the field of gangs and street culture. He is the youth and gang consultant for We Stand United Foundation. Weems helps support excellence by supporting his country, the needy, the ill, the hungry and the at-risk.

INTRODUCTION

This book is composed as a commemorative to honor and show my love, respect, support, and appreciation to our U.S. Military Armed Forces and its fallen heroes on the war on terrorism.

It is also composed to send my condolences to the families of the fallen heroes beyond spoken words of comfort, but by written words that I realize are a sure way to a lifeline through the cloudiness and clout of extreme mental and emotional suffering.

It is also the master key to open the locked doors, to free the spirit of impurities that hinder a person seeking tranquility within. It does more than alleviate agony or free the mind and heart of being in unwanted ambience. It allows a silent voice to be heard by a distant ear; an ear that would not have the gratification of hearing the voiced sentiments of one's appreciation and condolences.

I put together this collection of poetry to depict a picture much like an artist uses lines and shapes, but I with words that create powerful visual images that are movable in the mind's eye, that mingle with a gamut of deep emotions, and that create loving memories of why our fallen heroes have forfeited their lives. These brave soldiers have placed their lives on the line to protect the citizens and the land of the United States of America. Nothing we do can come close to thanking these heroes, but if nothing else, we can keep them in our hearts, prayers, and memories, and show our support for their many sacrifices.

Proceeds from this book are contributed to providing college scholarship trust funds for the kids of the fallen heroes of the war on terrorism, and to send care packages to the active duty U.S. military personnel fighting in the war.

So please show your support by purchasing an additional copy of this book for a family member or friend. You will be doing more than buying a beautiful commemorative piece of literature; you will also be showing your appreciation and saying Thank you to our U.S. military heroes.

TABLE OF CONTENTS

MAMA

Dear Mama,
My beloved mama, queen of the Nile,
queen of my heart,
it is I, your child and servant,
bringing forth words of gratitude to a queen.
Today started out as an average day,
the sun shining bright from what I could see
as I watched the birds fly by onto a destiny unknown,
and the ants search the ground for food unseen.

As I continue to watch God's creation take its course,
I realize how great His Majesty is.
Like your love, His love is unconditional and firm,
needing not to appear as a burning bush
or a man hung from a cross,
so pure, so real, yet unseen.

Mama, I was once in your womb,
free of sin and precious as a newborn dove
yet still free from the worldly things,
never knowing that my struggles shall be
as they are today, as your child and that strong
individual you raised me up to be.
You are still that loyal subject of my realm.
Yes, Mama, you are my queen, my love, my heart, my
Virgin Mary, my desire to strive and dream,
to fight through the struggles of all things.
It is because of your blood that flows through my veins,
that gives me that loving heart and that admirable face.
It is your smile that tells me your kingdom is mine,
as I reflect upon my thoughts.

Mama, I write to you from such a place,
held captive by those you tried to protect me from.
I write with a pain that is greater than such punishment,
but with a pain of not being able to be there with you.
But rest assured, strong I remain,
strong as the queen who raised me to be
the person I am today,
your loyal and trusted subject,
your child.

A MAN'S APPRECIATION TO
A QUEEN OF BRAVERY

How can your love be expressed for the U.S.
more than it already has?
Although your smile is the morning sunlight
that emits bright, and the sparkles in your eyes
are the stars in the sky at night
our heartbeat is what keeps your spirit alive
and inhaling the new morning breath keeps us
loving you to death.
Cookies and cakes, chocolate covered raisins and nuts
used to be the sugar dish to send a special touch.
Roses of red with long stems in a dozen
the sentiment of expression that says, I love you.
Gifts of clothes, gold chains or diamond rings
are usually how a man expresses
his feelings for a Queen.
Realizing you are worth more than such material
things,
for you are the rarest gem that gleams.
A flawless diamond, the Earth's Queen.
Through this valley of words and the effort I made
was all because I only wanted to say
thank you, Queen, for your bravery.

I MISS YOU

I believe in you, my love, my heart
My everything, my work of art.
I cherish you, I need you in my day
Sometimes I miss you more than words can say
Sometimes I feel like I am all alone.
You are the reason I'm never on my own.
Only you, my love, my inspiration,
Until the end of time, you are my motivation.
I miss you.

THE FIRE INSIDE

The blazing flames of a burning pain
Inside the soul of a Queen
Enslaved within a system
that is classified as a war mission
African, Native, Asian, Hispanic,
European descents. A Queen of the
same who created this nation of life.
Confined to inhuman conditions and
degraded beyond the physical surface
The burning fire inside the soul
keeps the heart warm and loving
It is you the Queen of Earth,
the foundation and elements
that keep the world continuing
Without you, the fire inside would die
and there is no life without the
Earth Queen
Which is you.

MY INSPIRATION

When thinking of you, I'm inspired
to be positive and upright
Thoughts of you help me to cope
even though you're out of sight
You are the light that illuminates my world
Gives me the strength to go on
And the endurance to remain strong
Your birth marked the inception of something special
Something I didn't quite understand then
Maybe a new beginning, maybe my means to an end
If only I could have seen the future through your eyes
Now that you're gone,
there is a remnant of you in my smile
I'm proud I helped produce a precious gift
For all the world to see A replica, a perfect
combination of your mother and me
No, I'm not presently there,
but I'm always aware of my pearl
My kings and queens of the world, my inspiration
My wonderful little boy, my beautiful little girl...

ON PATROL

Convinced within myself that my cause
is worth the leave of my family
I could hear my child scream
Never think about the distance
otherwise my heart bleeds
I miss my children
Lord knows, they miss me
My little ones are ill at ease
wondering am I home
But I'm half a world away
in the middle of a sandstorm
Each bump in the road
annoyed me even more
Patrolling in a Humvee
faithful marine corps
Shook from my daydream
when a bomb explodes
Vigilantes in dark streets
one never knows
The dead bodies odor
carries in the wind strong
Shoulder to shoulder
my unit patrols
The Humvee motor
revs on duty calls
I can't die tonight
got children at home
So I blot these worried thoughts and
focus on the task at hand
The enemy has plans
and I must defend my country
United We Stand

TRUE LOVE NEVER DIES

I'm having a hard time
I'm missing you in my heart
and in my mind
I miss all that you are to me,
but you will continue to be mine
I know you had to go away,
but it won't be for a lifetime
One day I will join you,
and I'll still be your bride
I'll never treat this love
as if it ever died
See, this ride is not over
It's very much alive
I'll accept this separation
and in this love take pride
It's because of your love
that I can't help but to survive
One day you'll look up in the heavens and see
my silhouette with adoration in my eyes
You'll smile and realize I'm with you,
for true love Never dies

DON'T CRY

Don't cry for me because I've done
only what I felt was right
Keep that in mind as you
burn those candles through the night
To cry for my soul would be
a waste of your precious tears
For I now reside in the kingdom of
the Heavenly Father with my peers
The love within your memories
should be caressed with a smile
Know that I gave my life
to protect the people of my country
And that should make you proud
The American soldier I am,
who now looks over his country from a cloud.

FRIENDSHIP OF THE LORD

Friendship is something to be held close to your
heart Hoping it will never be broken apart
Hoping the road up ahead is clear
Demolishing hate and crushing fear
Moving the world with just one hand
Counting every grain of sand
Flying high in the sky all the way to eternity
The Lord is sweeter than the sweetest spice
More than every grain of rice
Bigger than the biggest rock
Stronger than the strongest lock
That opens only with the key of memories
That keeps together you and me
Life ain't always what it seems
Sometimes it reminds us of a dream
When I'm worried and losing sleep
You keep me from falling weak
One thing I know for sure, my Lord
Life without you would be really hard
Each and every day that comes and goes
My love for you only grows

BREATH OF LIFE

We must learn to smile up at the sun
Allow its warm rays to smother the chills to the
world's ills
Seduce the morning freshness slowly
Capture it in our lungs for an intimate moment
Then release the Heavenly Father's breath back into
the atmosphere
So it can give the breath of life to another grieving
soul

LET HOPE REIGN

A time of peace and a time of war
The methodical splendor for what's in store
Massive clouds of hopeful deceit
Making my way toward being complete
Here I am in this dreary land of car bombs
An environment of hostility
unlike the country I call home
I can hear the resounding cries of people's souls
For liberty of war destruction fold
Now I know, I am not alone
for they're others who feel my pain
I can finally rest and let hope reign

LOVE FONDNESS

Distance to love fondness
Many milestones unaccomplished
Chest heavy with compelling burdens
Haunted memories
from carrying out a serpent's service
Questioning why I pledged allegiance to
America for which it stands
Wondering would America pledge
allegiance if I needed a hand
Distance to love fondness beyond
the identity of a soldier which I stand
Dearly missing the simple things in life
especially my family and friends

NO!

NO!

This is what I thought upon
hearing my child wasn't coming home.
This was the word I screamed when
I was told my child would be forever gone.
Do you feel my pain?
Or even care to understand?
I will recite this word until the day
that I can no longer stand.

ONE SMILE AT A TIME

We need you around, so
Don't be taken by surprise.
Don't let life get you down
Because every body cries.
We miss you dearly
Can't function right,
So take this sincerely,
Don't give up the fight.
Stay focused and on track,
And everything will be fine.
Everything will come back,
One smile at a time.

AN ANGEL THAT HAS BEEN SENT TO ME

She answered politely
with words I could not hear
With words that had been spoken,
but not heard by a distant ear
A journey into a world of eternity,
yet her voice had reached me
From words composed on paper
so gentle to the naked eye
Two strangers of the same,
many miles apart in different worlds
The caring thought of another,
brings what's separated by distance
Closer to each other
You have sent a gift
that has been sent by no other
Truly, you are an instrument of God's love
An angel that has been sent to do
what angels do above
I'll always cherish this thought
of your warm heart with a big hug
And by the same time tomorrow,
I'll still be holding on
To an angel that has been sent to me

A MOTHER WHO DIDN'T BELIEVE IN THE WAR

She was a Mother who didn't believe in the war
With a heart of a humanitarian that soared
A patriot for the country of stars and stripes
The embodiment of love
for all God's creation of life.
Though she despised the country's leader's lies
That sent her peers on a mission to take human lives
On their envoy many of them had died
That subjected family and friends
to a painful emotional ride.
Through the clouds of hopeful deceit
She pledged allegiance to world peace
She was a mother who didn't believe in the war
And yet she put on U.S. fatigues and became
A soldier to allow her love to soar.

WHISPERED

She was crying but only three,
a little Iraqi baby
Her mother was slaughtered
while she watched the blood leak
I was on duty but I felt such grief
because any little girl her age
shouldn't have to see
such hostilities.
Upon these hard streets
no one paid her mind
as she cried for me.
I was trained to be a soldier
but this scene is not me.
I hugged the little girl
and whispered, I'm sorry.

NO MATTER WHAT

If I could buy you the world,
I would purchase it
And name it after you.
If I could tell the future,
I would work overtime
To make your dreams come true.
If I could fly
I would capture the sky
And place it at your feet.
If I could kiss you
A million times, I would
Every time we meet.
You are my everything,
My hopes, my dreams, and all.
I dedicate my love to you,
Summer, spring, winter, and fall.
No matter what the future brings,
I welcome it with open arms
As long as we are together,
Life is worth living…
No matter what

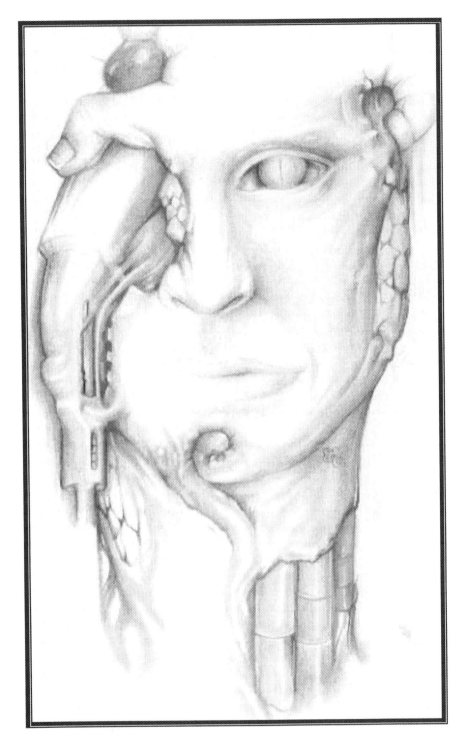

BRAVED THE UNKNOWN

The sand blown was blinding
Assumed another pose
I couldn't see the bullet
But in my chest a hole
In this world I live in
Difficult missions and visions
A mirage in the horizon
A helicopter flying
Paramedics ran to me
Surrounded my body's cold
They said I'll make it
But panic seized my bones
A stretcher unfolds
They tore off my clothes
Patched my wounds up
Flown to the hospital.
Alive impossible
These men I didn't know
No chance to say thank you
Only a belated thanks from the soul
I knew my time in war was much better than most
That day I met valor
When I braved the unknown

MY HANDSOME SON

Flesh of my flesh, blood of my blood
My precious son, separated but not torn
Completely safe in my heart's prayers and blessings
The successor to my struggle, my hope for the future
My continuing strength as I grow weak
Surely God has blessed me with you
A continuance of hope in the lap of darkness
My handsome son I love you wholeheartedly
Our love will always be connected as one
And you will always remain
My handsome son

DUTY

Upon a rooftop, I lay on my belly
Haven't showered, haven't shaved
My gun I hold steady
They ran the streets bloody
With one eye closed
I observed my enemy inside my gun scope
Target was dead center
So I squeezed my trigger
I was a doctor in my country
Today I'm a soldier
My bird's eye perch gave me confirmed kills
Struggled with all this dying
Is this God's will?
I was told to keep firing
On my stomach I lay still.

HAPPY BIRTHDAY

To a very special person
On a very special day
I wish you many happy moments
So your smile won't go away.
Today is your day.
Remember that I am with you
Even though I may not be there.
I can't believe that you are a year older
One more year of time.
Take a moment to reflect on the things
That make you smile and brighten your day.
And remember, I love you more than life itself,
And more than words can say.

REMINISENCE

We reminisce at repertory times,
on things from the past
From the wonderful moments we shared
and unconditional love
That joins us as one
Chained as metal locks
without keys or combinations
To separate what is so tightly connected
as you and I.

Although we may not recall our first kiss
which you assured me took place
By your tender lips
while held tight in your warm embrace
Your smile has magic sparkles
to brighten up my lonely days
And the enchanting quality
to electrify my impulsiveness
To what is so real,
so beautiful in existence.

My heart beats for your love
The blood that flows through my veins
is the mechanism puzzle
That keeps your love safe within
As the air you exhale,
I choose to breathe
A part of you I refuse to let leave.

My life circulates around you,
held tight in the earth's atmosphere
Flowing naturally through its course
Creating memories of good and worse
As we reminisce at repertory times
on things from the past
Surely our love will always last

GOD'S GREATEST GIFT TO ME

God's greatest gift to me is He
A colored diamond, a rare piece
A one of a kind precious jewel
A jewel that we find ourselves seeking out
Its hand in friendship and wealth
For the hereafter
A gift that is priceless within its world
And has the power to strengthen us
From separation and shame
And sin's temptation to worldly things
For I give thanks, for now I know
God's greatest gift to me, is He who helped me grow
God's greatest gift to me is He

FRIENDS

You are my friends,
forever and a day
You were there for me and America,
no matter they say.
Friend's forever, because
we've been through thick and thin.
When you pledged your life to America
And traveled the journey to foreign land
To let the world know we will win
Because United we stand
I am here for you,
Just like you were there for me.
We have to help each other
Today, tomorrow, for eternity.
Friends forever, because
True friendships are few.
I just want to thank God
For blessing me with friends like you.

A JUST HEART

I stand firmly with a just heart
Without fear of the oppressors of the earth
Who are the believers of idols and falsehoods
I am blessed by the Supreme Ruler
Of all elements and composed substances
I am blessed by the King of mankind
The original and only God of mankind
Who is the most gracious and merciful
To all who believe in Him
The Creator of creations is where my faith remains
With the beat of my heart
Staying in His grace with His harmony

QUENCH MY SOUL THIRST

Quench my soul thirst with freedom essence
Unmask the waterfall of love and peace
Explore the realm of my American descendant spirit
To see the red white and blue in me,
Educate my conscience with world history
Supply my footing with stability
Nourish my heart with Mother Nature`s breast
And watch an American soldier manifest

CHERISH THE DAY

Take the time to romance the morning
Feel its sun upon your face
And as day turns to evening
Watch the stars fall into place
Cuddle the moon with memories
Of those that warm the heart
For the world is God's canvas
And you his living work of art
Each of us is an element
Within this canvas of life
Some will struggle under heavy burdens
While others walk will be light
Inhale deeply the atmosphere's breath
That oxygenates the soul
Then release it back into the sky
To ease your worries of the untold
Let not the journey overwhelm you
For anxiety will set in place
Take the time to romance the morning
Feel its sun upon your face

WHEN I FELL IN LOVE WITH YOU

Maybe it was the first time
I was blessed with the sight of your face.
Maybe it was our conversation,
Your intelligence, your style, your grace.
Maybe it was the fact that
I could not get you out of my mind.
Maybe it was your beauty,
You were passionate and kind.
Maybe it was at that moment
When I realized I needed you in my life.
Maybe it was when I made up my mind
That you would be a perfect mate.
I can't point out the exact moment
When I fell in love with you.
All I know is that I love you, I love you,
And my love for you is true.

TO BE ONE

She walked into my day
A wreath of pleasure
Her silhouette was many shapes
Charmed beyond measure
She was heat when I was cold
Sewing threads in my soul
So many sad songs sung
Pacing to and fro
The knowledge of angels
Only ripened her fruit
Enchanting elegance
But a handful in truth
Her wants, impractical
Her mood, impossible
I overcame these obstacles
And found that heaven is tangible
She was bashful so I built her a castle
She stood by the window
Whispering it's beautiful
Far off saw the meadows
The trees and waterfalls
And that very night she sang me a song
Her love was musical
Silk to skin we lay upon the sheets
Then fairytales were written
Entrusted with a gift
I began to paint a picture
And that's what it's like
To be one with Mother Nature....

HEAL IN TIME

Your spirit is beautiful, blissful and kind
Sweet to the heart, comfort to the mind
Your smile brings joy and happiness just the same
But on the other side of that smile
exists nothing but pain
When emotions are neglected by those that we love,
The other side of emotions causes us to experience
Sadness of love, which we refuse to admit
When we are really in pain
because of this there will be times
when you must endure love's defeat
Believe in God He will keep us from becoming weak
Your spirit is still beautiful, blissful and kind
Never let that go, for the pain will heal in time

AMERICA IN WHICH WE STAND

Chaos struck our nation through infiltration
A deeply motivated hatred by a foreign nation
An attempt to destroy the land of the free
PLEEEASE!
The United States of America is who we be
Just wait until you feel the wrath of destruction that
we bring
We will do more than what your imagination could
ever conceive
We will exterminate all of the terrorists
And those who pose a threat to the citizens of
American land
The red, white and blue
America in which we stand

AMERICAN HEROES

Today we want to express our appreciation
To our favorite men and women on earth.
You are a special part of our lives,
Nothing can ever display what you are worth.
Today, tomorrow, in the future we may need you
And we know you will be there
We know sometimes we may not show it,
But deep inside we care.
You are important, soldiers,
We need you in our lives each day.
We are forever in debt to you,
More than words can ever say.
So here's to you, our American heroes,
Recognizing how important you are to us.
We love you as much a heart can feel
And as far as the eye can see.

VISIONS OF MYRIADS

Sometimes I ask, "What is it all about?"
As I stare heavenward, lookin' within the clouds
We live our lives praying to make the right decisions
Another soldier entered the realm to become a vision
Many have cried for their souls
But the myriads continue to move within the folds
On bended knee, I bow my head in reverence
The visions of myriads gallop on
As their memories serve as heir apparent

MY ANGEL

I miss you in ways you may not perceive
My heart has the sound of a second beat
When the thought of you comes to mind
My soul hasn't smiled since the absence of your loving
spirit
I'm incomplete without my angel, which is you
What motivated me, you were a part of
Although my outer surface may not show
The contents that my heart holds
It knows
It knows what others are blind to
It knows
You are my angel

THE SOLDIER

The greatest men that ever moved
came from a soldier's wounds.
Their hearts survive the booms
of war when the night looms.
Despite these conditions,
our men complete the missions.
The soldiers never yield,
learning new lessons.
Roaming the battlefields
Generals became pleased
determined beyond grief.
Humanity needs Marines
and Army and Navy.
Air Force guard the skies.
Coast Guard provide supplies
the war may never die.
Cannons. . ...fire
into the night.
Oh such vigorous minds
these stars and stripes! As I unraveled the flag
that keeps our hope alive.
These are the men
that have earned the right to cry.

APPRECIATE EARTH

We must find a way
to climb the clouds.
Drink the rain,
kiss the sky on our way
Inhale the air
to release the pain.
Feel the freshness of its breeze.
Clinch onto the sun,
the moon, the stars,
Hug the atmosphere,
that seems so far.
Love the galaxy for all within.
A galaxy that has always
been a friend.

YOU LOVED AMERICA SO MUCH

You loved America so much
Enough to willingly sacrifice your life
And the liberties of the daily pleasures and activities
That warm your heart with a smile
You loved America so much
Enough to willingly abandon your family and friends
To protect its land, citizens, values and history
You loved America so much
You pledged your loyalty and life to fight
So that the American citizen's dreams, goals and
desires
Could live on without worries of threats
You loved America so much
You gave, you, for America

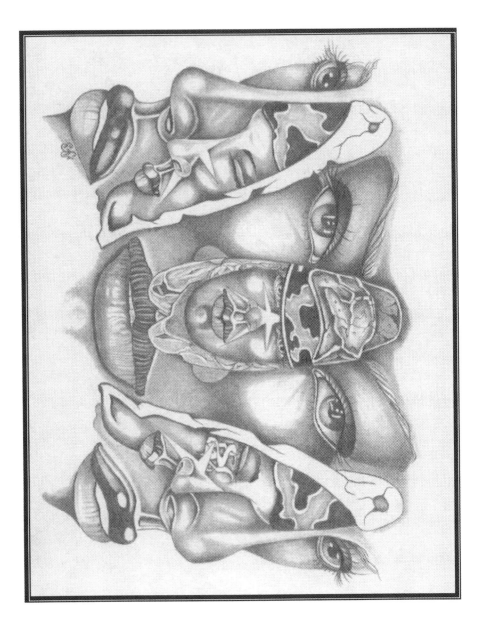

LOVE

Love is the word that identifies you care,
above all, love would always be there.
Overall there remain three words that define love,
without one, love could not be,
the true meaning of love exists only with the three.
Versed well in heart with patience, devotion, and
dedication,
mix the three and understand the true meaning
of love, as it should be.
Care not how hopeless the outlook may seem,
or how deeply seated may be the trouble
with the true meaning of love,
when you have the three mixed into one,
you can't be deceived.
Even though the word love is used
by so many that yet understand,
perhaps semblance might deceive the truth,
by a word which is used so freely.

TO MY FRIEND

To my friend:
We've only known one another for a short time.
Yet we are like brothers; peas from the same pod,
lions from the same pack, stuck in a modern day
Roman's den,
forced to fight, forced to kill or be killed,
taken from our jungle and caged,
unable to move as we see fit,
once kings of our jungle hunting prey,
now reduced to being prey.
Who is it that is able to cage two such as us?
Able to cause us to rely on handouts,
to be beaten mentally and abused physically?
What manner of beast has us trapped,
and at the snap of a whip doing flips through a ring of
fire?
My friend, we've hunted together in the past,
and now we have become the hunted.
But rest assured, my friend, we shall some day be free,
free to roam the open plains, free to choose a mate.
But for now, old friend, rest your mind,
for what it stores they cannot take.
Dream, my friend, dream well,
for tomorrow is a new day and
we mustn't let the enemy find us tired,
lest we give up and become one of the losers.
Rest now, old friend,
for memories of old are all we have.
But no matter what, we shall still be friends.

A WOMAN'S VALENTINE'S DAY

A woman's Valentine's Day should be much more
than a single day a man finds to be special,
to value one's love and appreciation.
A woman's Valentine's Day should offer
more than a moment of thanks
over a candlelight dinner,
a few red rose petal's underneath a bottle of wine,
with a box of chocolate hearts that say you are mine.

A woman's Valentine's Day should be more
than a hot bubble bath near a burning fireplace,
a hot oil body massage and sweet words
to fill an empty space.
A woman's Valentine's Day should be every day,
from the moment she wakes and all in between,
until she lies down to sleep as the earth's Queen.
A woman's Valentine's Day should be every day,
for she is the key that brings life to all things.
So remember...
A Woman's Valentine's Day.

MOTHER

You were there when I took
My first breath of air,
When I took my first step
You gave me love and care.
You cured my colds, my attitudes,
And even my nasty ways.
You protected me through storm nights
And many rainy days.
My provider, my teacher,
No woman could ever take your place.
No sight is more beautiful to me
Than to see a smile on your face.
You are my motivation,
You have taught me so many things,
I will always love you,
No matter what the future brings.
My mother, My Mom,
the lady I love, respect, and admire.
My love for you is everlasting
My love will never expire.
I appreciate you, I admire you,
I will remember what you said
I could never repay you for
What you did for me,
But let me start by saying
I love you.

YOU?

Honey, sweet potato pie, butterscotch, sugar pops,
Chocolate, muffin, Gummy Bears, gum drops,
Peppermint, strawberries, licorice, hot tamales,

Cup cakes, cherry pie, blueberries, Tootsie Rolls,
Bubble Yum, Now and Laters, Mike N'Ikes, Jello,
Pumpkin pie, Twinkies, jelly beans, Bit-o-Honey,

Milky Way, candy cane, cotton candy, Snickers,
Carrot cake, pecan pie, Chick-o-Stick, cookies,
Ice cream, skittles, M&Ms, Honey Bun…

I give up…
Nothing on this earth
Is as sweet as you!

I APPRECIATE YOUR WORTH

A single rotation of the earth
is not enough time to appreciate your worth,
for what you bring into this world;
life, a beautiful child to replenish this world:
You are the essence of the world's existence,
the door to life, a source of salvation
and the most important element that creates history.
Your gentle touch is like a light cool breeze
of air on a hot summer day that brings comfort to the
soul.
As your love flows unconditionally,
it flows like ocean waves to places unknown.
Who knows how deep it goes...who knows?
You are the morning sunrise and the tears from your
eyes
are the raindrops that fall from the skies.
Your smile is like the moon at night,
that night star that shines over me so bright,
the period of light between dawn and night.
My heartbeats express my appreciation
and gratitude for your existence.
Although my spoken words may not reflect that form of
expression,
if you could read my private journal
then would you understand the love I hold within
and just how much I appreciate your worth.
And I hope that some day we could become close
friends...

A BIRTHDAY WISH

A Birthday wish we all have made
over candles burning upon a cake.

Saying a silent wish before taking a deep breath
to blow over the sugar dish.

Wondering when we would be granted
that Birthday wish.

Ready to dig into its sweetness,
to taste that we have wished over,
that seals our faith.

Years continue to pass,
would this Birthday wish be like the last,
or have we received a better wish?

A blessing to see another Birthday,
to continue to make a Birthday Wish.

DECEIVED

Every inch of my body has become bruised
traveling over the bumpy roads
with constant betrayal of friends.
I feel like Job delivered into the hands of the
wicked,
unannounced without explanation,
exhausted, impossible to sleep,
cramped constantly without a place to stretch,
traveling alone, suffering in misery without a
voice that could be heard.
Words with hope to an endless dream,
dreams promised by family and friends,
pain and agony traveling free through my tired
body.
You have deceived me, like Eve did onto Adam,
without explanation, left wondering,
pondering on the stars hovering in the
atmosphere.
Where are you when I'm in need?
A letter would be nice, a hug would be even
better,
some support would be immaculate beyond
all that could be offered in my time of need.
What good does it do me by you drifting on past
memories,
when it's so clear that I am in need of your divine
services,
to help free what needs to be free,
free from betrayal, free from pain and agony?
Deliver me from suffering by showing me

that you haven't deceived me in my time of need,
and your presence would not only be just a
memory,
a memory of thinking of me,
but a friend who is there for a friend in time of
need.
Tell me that I haven't been deceived,
by showing me that my belief is just a belief,
and you are still with me.

I MOVE LIKE A CAT

I move like a cat...
always watching with intense patience...
very silent with light purrs that have great meanings...
aware of all that is around my circumference...
creeping slowly trying not to be noticed.
I'm quick on my feet when I must be...
and have no problem climbing objects to reach a safe
location...
uncomfortable around too many people...
hugging only those who I'm used to feasting with.
Caution within my psychological mind...
realizing life is not measured by time...
but is measured by your actions and deeds...
if you must stay alive.
That's why I move like a cat...
always watching with intense patience....

PONDERING AMONG THE SKY

Underneath a blazing red sky,
clouds of red and white pass by
through the vision of love that twinkles in my eye
to the sight of a ruby red sky.

The sound of thunder is the beat of my heart
as I stand, glancing into the sky, pondering in the dark.
As cool winds caress my body with chilly thrills,
to an intense moment to what I really feel.

As a burning star shines over me so bright,
I wonder; could that be a sign from my future wife?
As I continue to gaze deep into the sky
I notice a beautiful red moon my eyes see at night.

So I ponder at the moment in wonder,
in amazement of the sight of a ruby red sky
that I see through the vision of my eyes.
Could it be a sign from my future wife?
Could it be she's among the ruby red sky?

UNCLEAR

Through the eyes I see clear,
with images that are depicted as they are.
A vision to my assurance to what is around my aura.
The mind seems to stray on its own,
with thoughts that are unclear.
Emotions tend to flare from visions that are not really
there.
Are the skies truly blue or gray?
Are the skies truly blue or gray?
Are the skies truly blue or gray,
or is it just too foggy out to really say?
What is it that has my vision unclear today,
questioning my eyes to what seems to be in front of
them?
Would it be that my eyes are deceiving me,
leaving my vision unclear to reality?
Or could it be that it's just too foggy out to really see?
Whatever it may be, it still remains all unclear to me.

YOU HOLD THE KEY

You hold the key.
I welcome you into my life openly and freely
since introducing you into my heart.
I patiently await your tender grace each day.
So often you cool my spirits with your lovely smile.
Your physical presence I long to hold for a while.
To take you into my firm gentle embrace,
would fill my life's loneliest space.
You hold the key to free my soul,
adding freshness to my life that never grows old.
Your divine, tender touch is something I yearn for.
There is so much beauty when I look into your eyes,
a journey across heaven's crystal white skies.
You hold the key, of this I assure you.
There is no other in this present world
whom I adore more than I do you.
If I could have one wish come true,
I would wish that I would never be separated from you.
For it is true, you hold the key.

PRICELESS LOVE

Like a gentle breeze my love will cool you
My love is honest
It will never try to fool you.
Like sunshine, my love will bring you heat
My love is real, my love is complete.
Like your smile, your touch,
My love is real.
My love for you is as strong as steel.
Like tomorrow, I am never too far away
My love cares for you each day.
No one on earth can take the place of you.
You inspire my essence
You make me feel new.
My love for you is priceless,
It's not for sale.
Your secrets are safe with me,
I will never tell.

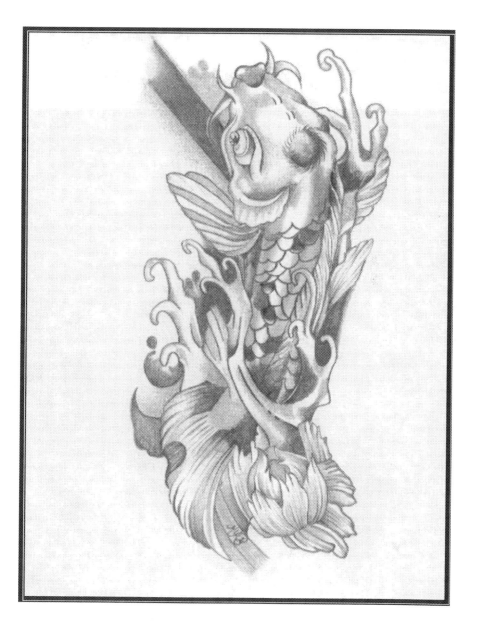

AUNTY LOVE

Your love is so unique, always around when I'm in
need.
You teach me things I must know, and guide me as I
grow.
Your womanly touch is so unique, it uplifts me when
I'm weak.
You are my friend when I have no other,
and at times you take the place of my mother.
We speak in words that you and I can only understand,
a code between us two to a master plan.
When you are around I have not one worry,
for you will make sure everything is okay.
You cook when I'm hungry,
you wash when my clothes need cleaning,
we spend time together and share some of our deepest
secrets.
Nothing I do is wrong in your eyes,
you stay down with me, even when you know that I'm
lying.
You would fight hand to hand on my side,
that's how I know you'll be with me from the hand of
time.
Aunty Love...

AN UNCLE'S LOVE

As a child, you were always around,
you came and went but always could be found.
You always made sure that you checked up on me.
When the weekends came, I would be headed to your
house
to spend the night with your family.
We would sit and eat, smile and jive,
and listen to you tell stories of the past experiences of
your life.
Your jokes kept people laughing all throughout the
day,
at night it was also the same way.
We would sit at the piano as I watched you play,
you would teach me songs that were way before my
days.
Every weekend we were sure to spend together,
pulling the boat out of the driveway, headed out to go
fishing.
Money you have never cherished, always free hearted
and very giving,
your word you were sure to keep, an honest man,
anyone would see.
Your personality cannot be matched, for you are one
of a kind,
and I'm sure someone has already told you that.
In my heart you have your own special place,
that I shall cherish for the rest of my days.
An uncle's love should be no other way.
An uncle's love...I cherish to the end of my days...
An Uncle's Love

DISTANCE EAR

A distance ear is an ear that can hear at a distance.
The sounds of words travel many ways,
as the air moves throughout the earth undetected,
flowing freely.
Distance has no limits to its destination
and the ear is not biased to what can be heard from a
distance.
As for those who may not be in your presence,
such distance does not mean that they cannot hear you,
for word travels in many ways.
To a Distance Ear.....

RAINDROPS

Raindrops soft and wet upon my chest.
Serene liquid, atmosphere splendor.
Raindrops fall soft and tender,
splashing puddles, hugs and cuddles.
Love is in the air, clouds filled with sustenance
for the earth's surfaces.
Creation bonds, responds to the element's chilly thrills.
Raindrops continue to spill,
giving hope to the world's ills.
The sky cries because the earth's so dry.
Raindrops moisten our unhappy lives.....

BREATHE WITH ME

Breathe with me
Exhale the pain of disappointments you struggle with
Find your heartbeat that hides behind the shadows
Deep in the darkness within
Inhale the fresh air that is me
Let my love be the new sound of your heartbeat
If only, you could breathe with me

SOLUTION

Complex situations
worse than a famine
They wrote a constitution
but confusing things have happened
The path not open,
roadside bombs exploden
Freedom the people hoping,
in the rumble of wreckage smoken
Circumstances difficult,
the violence been perpetual
Since these criminals,
making rebuilding impossible
Lingering death I mention,
among religious dissention
Creator proof I imagine,
in the land which loves fighting
But there's some negotiations,
to democratic solutions
But not too many listen,
yelling revolution
Never been in the position,
a soldier was thinking
Suppressed his expression,
duty calls while others sleeping
He walked the meanest streets,
five thousand miles away
They spoke a language he didn't know
To his last day he stayed....

MY LOYAL HAND

My loyal hand is blessed by the will of the Lord
It has the power to caress the evil spirits away
For love and evil clash
Hate runs from love's sweet chord
The gentle touch of life's sweet bliss
Evaporates venom with a holy kiss
As my loyal hand remains blessed
By the will of the Lord

BLESS THEM

All the goodness in the world
Must be poured in this country
I can't understand the debate politically
Do you want me home
After all my blood spilled?
I died for a cause
And a belief that must not fail
I'm watching from a distance
In another solar system
I haven't died for nothing
So don't you try leaving
The war stands for something
Politicians you better listen
We shall prevail, my comrades are staying
God bless them

WE STAND UNITED 1

When that morning arrived
Alas it burned my mind
Crucified and sacrificed
A tragedy brings a sign
I saw the eagle rise
Some people thought he died
Despite the flames and smoke
Sometimes it's hard to climb
But it's endless to the sky
Oh shine eagle of mine
I'm inclined to be diving
In a world beyond this time
Overcame mortality with cause
That made me fly
We stand united for all
Those who died

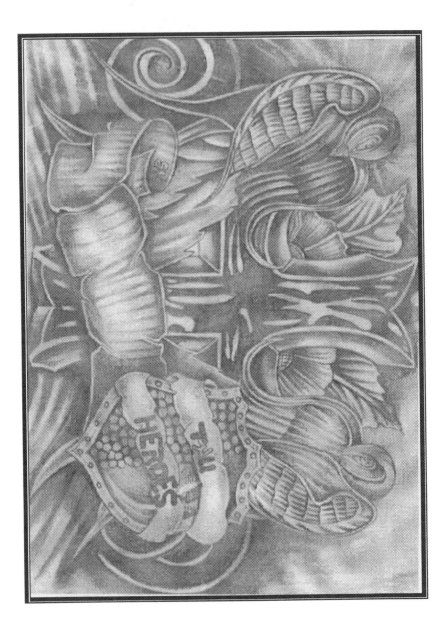

UNDERNEATH THE SUN

Underneath the sun fearless secrets
rest on the earth's surface.
Vision is not a necessity.
Sight has no purpose.
Birth offers no identity
to a particle without hope
that moves freely as the air.
Dreams are not yet understood
of an identity that's not there.
History shall soon explain,
and I shall know my identity.
Underneath the sun,
fearless secrets rest
on the earth's surface.

A SOLDIER'S PROMISE

Every crooked turn in the city that burns
makes me appreciate the country I serve.
For now I meditate and pray about my fate.
I'm from the United States;
a welcome home is not too late.
My friend died today,
I didn't know what to do,
had his family's picture in the barracks
by mine, too.
A somber spirit engulfed my unit,
a rifle with a helmet was placed in the pavement.
He didn't have to go, you know
it could have been me.
It was time to patrol,
so I walked his beat.
In loving memory,
my respect to his family
promise I won t come home
until his mission's complete.

CAN YOU HEAR ME?

Can you hear me as I enter the air?
Do you feel me kissing your neck?
When you know there's no one really there
Can you feel me tasting your sweetness?
That you produce so naturally
Caressing your lips with the warmth of the air's rafter
Speak if it's not fair that you can't hold me when I'm
holding you
Or touch me when I'm so near
Caressing your nakedness, as beautiful as you are
The smell of your essence excites my senses
My heart races with chills as I overwhelm you with my
presence
Every time you inhale, you inhale a part of me
What seems so unreal is only unreal to those who
disbelieve
A disbelief in what can't be seen
Through the vision of a pair of eyes
A dream is how to bring your sight, a visual of me
To the soul of a man who roams the air free
Can you hear me as I enter the air?
Loving you, when there's no one really there...
Can you hear me?

AGONY

My expressions flow freely like the Mississippi River.
The pen that I write with is my only lifeline
through the cloudy and clout of agony to reach
humanity.
My thoughts seem caged and contained like my
physical movement,
suppressed, restricted and restrained from their natural
course of nature by the stony walls that impose upon
my liberty.
My only sunshine is from a ceiling light
that emits its insemination of rays upon my body,
and my fresh air circulates through a ventilation system
and seeps its way back beneath the cracks of my door.
My sunset is at a flick of a switch that brings complete
darkness,
with old memories of the past that end with thoughts of
"ifs and ands."
My body feels internally bruised,
beaten and worn by the lack of nourishment,
hunger pains hinder my motivation to push forward
with future goals,
words have no meaning to the ears of the oppressor.
Violence is the only solution to obtain their attention,
to hear the softly spoken words of a plea.
Yet I sit caged like a wild beast,
frustrated and hurting from the deep mental pain,
and blaming myself as if I had done wrong
rather than protect myself from physical harm.
Am I wrong for protecting me?
If so, let it be. I shall always stand strong
when it comes to protecting me.

M-16

I think that you'll be missed the most.
We've been through a great deal together
and it goes deeper than guard post.
You did your best in protecting me,
but everything must come to a close eventually.
Who will possess you now?
Who will partner with you?
Whoever it may be, may your mission be a successful
one.
Who would have thought
my last loved one would be a gun?

IN MEMORY OF THE AMERICAN SOLDIER

War of preparation
Chaos coming from two separate nations
Fighting for currency and power
Watching each other every minute of the hour
Satellite dishes trinkets and gadgets
Metaphorically an electronic beauty pageant
The lady with the best dress wins
And for the loser with no friends to cater to her whims
The hell just begins.

Faces torn half off
Sprays of blood when they cough
Droplets of the same liquid fall on his lip and chin
He reaches for his M-16, his loyal friend
He carries the spirit of a true soldier within
There is a hole in his jaw, but he still puts on a grin
Cocks back the firing pin
Squeezes the trigger and lets the bullets fly
until the clip hits the end.

He was taught that his rifle is his wife,
his mother, his brother
Manufactured in America
It shoots like no other
It rips people apart in a treacherous way
The combination of this man and his gun
Come together as one to defend the USA.

Total destruction in the sight to his past
Enough blood from his wounds
to run him a bath
He feels his life slipping away
It flashes before his eyes to his past
And the blackness of his vision
assures him he has been had
All that he worked for
to this point is all gone
He gave his life for his country
and now his name shall live on
In Memory of the American Soldier.....

DEAR CREATOR, I HAVE COME

The beat of my heart is like the beat of an African
drum
It reminds me of my energy, also of my mortality
The essence which forces my mortal limbs into motion
to and fro
One beat, two beats three beats, four
Continuing in rhythm until the body is no more
Unknown to me, my physical time is up
I endure my moments, thankful for their existence
I thrive to survive
While experiencing what's real can quite possible be
an illusion
My heartbeat enables that door to remain open, but
inconclusive
Once I cross the threshold and that beat is no more
And behind me closes the door to the unknown
Farewell will be my response to the beat of the drum
As my soul flees and my limbs go numb
I embrace eternity
Dear Creator, I have come

BLACK ORCHID

This flower that I hold
Oddly suggested in color and shape
Can't be appreciated by your sight, because
You've lost that visual embrace
This flower that I hold
Sweet and decadent in odor
Can't be appreciated by your nostrils, because
You'll need the sense of smell no more
This flower that I hold
Delicate and highly cultivated
Will be laid on your grave
Despite the fact
You can't appreciate it!

UNSEPARATED LOVE

I held you in my arms to keep you close to my heart.
Even though you traveled on,
memories of our love keep me holding on.
I feel your presence watching over me daily,
listening to my spoken words as I send you my
undying love.
I can feel your soul caressing my heart.
You're everywhere I go
that's how I know you are still holding on.
When my time is over and my chores are through,
I will come to heaven to spend eternity with you.

WE STAND UNITED

We stand united but orbit in solitude
Explored so many ways
to express our love for you
Sacred like the burning bush of Moses on fire
We remember you soldiers forever our desire
You've remained in our vision
Corey Miller was saying
This book is the language of
God when he's praying
Many will never know the few inside this fold
Such as Demetrius McClendon, a living inferno
The memories of all the fallen shall never be
forgotten
Imagined this happening Kimberline "Black
Diamond" Johnson
The eternal was stirring in Mister Eugene Weems
Ideas reoccurring never gave up the dream
Medicine for the sick poetry was but a gift
Your battles are important to the team that made this
The freshness of dawn began to swell by God
We stand united with all the U.S. troops abroad

THE WIFE

Her beauty was not the reason I said I do.
Memories of long talks about nothing at all
Through the winter, spring, summer and fall.
I wasn't pressured to be anything other then myself.
The excitement of happiness was always there.
Her beauty was not the reason I said I do.
Unconditional love is what kept us
two connected as one
I knew that she was meant for me,
that's why we became a family.
Her beauty was not the reason I said I do....

IN MEMORY OF OUR FALLEN HEROES

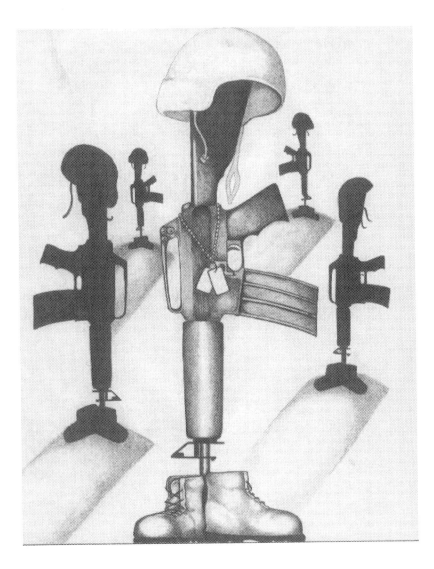

Attention Readers

After reading this book you can express your love and gratitude to the troops and or to the families of the fallen heroes by writing how you feel as well as your appreciation and condolences. Your note will not only be read by the troops and their families, but by millions of Americans.

Please be brief and forward your letter to:

United We Stand (Letters)
1541 Golden Sea Ln
North Las Vegas, NV 89032